Undeniably Guilty

A True Story

Positively Forgiven

CHARLOTTE PERRY-BRIGGS

KP PUBLISHING COMPANY

ISBN: 978-1-960001-80-1 (Hardcover)
ISBN: 978-1-960001-81-8 (Paperback)
ISBN: 978-1-960001-82-5 (eBook)

Library of Congress Control Number: Pending

Editor: KP Publishing Editorial Services
Cover Design: Juan Roberts, Creative Lunacy
Literary Director: Sandra Slayton James

Scriptures marked KJV are taken from the KING JAMES VERSION (KJV): KING JAMES VERSION, public domain.

Scripture taken from the New King James Version®. Copyright © 1982 by Thomas Nelson. Used by permission. All rights reserved.

Disclaimer:
The events, characters, and facts described in this book are based on the legal proceedings, including the outcomes of the initial trial and the retrial. While every effort has been made to present accurate information, specific details have been included for narrative clarity and reader understanding. This work is not intended to serve as a comprehensive legal record.

Published by:

KP Publishing Company
Publisher of Fiction, Nonfiction & Children's Books
Las Vegas, NV 89117
www.kp-pub.com

Printed in the United States of America

CONTENTS

DEDICATION

I lovingly dedicate this book to the cherished memory of our beloved son, Charles Emmanuel Briggs, whose light continues to guide and inspire us. To my husband, Charlie, and our beautiful daughters, Charlena, Charlynnae, and Charmaine, thank you for your unwavering strength, love, and resilience that sustain our family.

I also dedicate this book to:

- **Our extended family:** You have remained an integral part of our journey, bound together by love and the memory of Charles. Though I cannot name each of you individually, please know that you hold a special place in our hearts. Your presence is a testament to the enduring power of family, and we love you deeply.

- **Gary and Jody:** You entered our lives as strangers and became steadfast pillars of support in the aftermath of an unthinkable tragedy. Your willingness to stand with us, especially during the trials, is a gift we will never forget.

Your compassion brought light to some of our darkest days.

- **Mothers who have lost a child to violence:** To each of you, I extend my heartfelt prayers that you may find healing in the profound act of forgiveness. May this book be a reminder that even in the depths of pain, there is hope and the possibility of freedom through grace?

May *Undeniably Guilty, Positively Forgiven* honor Charles Emmanuel Briggs' legacy and serve as a beacon of hope, healing, and inspiration for all who navigate the path of loss and redemption.

PREFACE

Losing a child to murder is a tragedy that defies words—a pain so profound it feels as if your very soul has been torn apart. As a mother who has walked this unprecedented path, I know the depths of grief, the overwhelming anger, and the suffocating sense of helplessness that consumes you. It is a wound that changes the course of your life forever.

In the aftermath of such devastation, it is natural to want to retreat, to shut out the world, and to dwell in the darkness of your pain. The reality of such a loss can feel unbearable, leaving you questioning how to go on. I write this preface with a heart full of empathy, understanding, and hope, for I want to share a truth that has brought me peace in the midst of my sorrow: the power of forgiveness.

Forgiveness is not easy. It feels unthinkable when faced with the enormity of the crime that has taken your child. But forgiveness is not about excusing or forgetting—it is about freeing yourself from the chains of anger and bitterness that can imprison your heart. It is a process, often slow and painful, but one that offers the promise of healing and the possibility of reclaiming your life from the grip of despair.

Through forgiveness, I found a way to honor my son's memory—not by holding on to the pain but by allowing love, grace, and peace to take root in my heart once again. Forgiveness does not diminish the depth of your loss or the magnitude of the injustice; it simply gives you a chance to live with purpose, even in the face of devastating grief.

As you navigate this difficult journey, know that your pain, while profound, is not eternal. Over time, the sharp edges of grief will soften. Though the ache may never fully disappear, you will find moments of light breaking through the darkness. You are not alone on this path. Others have walked this path before you, and there are resources and communities to help guide and support you. Take the time you need to grieve, to reflect, and to begin to envision a future where hope and healing coexist with your loss. You are not alone.

This book is my offering to you—a testament to the resilience of the human spirit and the transformative power of forgiveness. I pray that in these pages, you will find comfort, strength, and a glimmer of hope for your own journey. Remember, even in the face of undeniable guilt, forgiveness is possible, and it can transform your life.

Even in the face of undeniable guilt, forgiveness is possible. It is not an easy path, but it can lead to healing and peace. Please consider that forgiveness is not about excusing or forgetting—it is about freeing yourself from the chains of anger and bitterness that can imprison your heart.

> *"A person can be undeniably guilty and positively forgiven."*
>
> Charlotte Perry-Briggs

INTRODUCTION

January 10, 2022

"Dear Charlotte, I got your card today. Happy New Year to you and your family. I can't tell you how much it means to me that you took the time and wrote me. There is not a day that goes by where I don't think about Charles and how sorry I am for what I did."

— Garrett Adams

The letter came like a whisper, cutting through the noise of grief that had become my constant companion. It wasn't just words scrawled on paper—it was a reminder of the unbearable pain that had changed my life forever and a spark of something I had been clinging to: forgiveness.

On August 23, 2014, my world shattered. Garrett Adams, a young Caucasian man, murdered my only son, Charles Emmanuel Briggs. My son was gone. The devastation was incomprehensible, and the weight of my loss felt unbearable.

In the aftermath, I grappled with questions I never thought I'd face. How could I go on without Charles? How could I forgive the man who tore my family apart? Yet, as the days turned into nights, one truth became inescapable: forgiveness wasn't just an option—it was my lifeline.

Psychologists define forgiveness as a conscious, deliberate decision to release resentment or vengeance toward someone who has harmed you. But for me, it was more than that. Forgiveness wasn't about excusing Garrett's actions or forgetting what had happened. It was about finding a way to reclaim my peace and trust in God's plan.

When Garrett took Charles's life, I began praying for forgiveness almost immediately—not because it felt natural or easy, but because I knew it was necessary. My faith compelled me to remember Jesus' example on the cross. As He suffered, He prayed,

"Father, forgive them, for they know not what they do"
Luke 23:34 (KJV)

Those words echoed in my heart, even as anger and sorrow threatened to consume me. I discovered that forgiveness is not a single moment but a journey. It's a daily choice to release anger, even when bitterness feels justified. It's a process of praying for someone who caused your deepest pain, even when you do not feel strong enough to say the words.

"But if ye forgive not men their trespasses, neither will your Father forgive your trespasses."

Matthew 6:15 (KJV)

This journey was not mine alone. My husband, my daughters, and I each faced our own battles with grief and forgiveness. While our paths looked different, we shared one common truth: holding onto anger would only prolong our suffering. Forgiveness became our collective lifeline, allowing us to rebuild, day by day, with God's grace as our foundation.

Undeniably Guilty, Positively Forgiven is not just the story of my loss. It is a testimony of faith, resilience, and the decision to forgive the unforgivable. This book is for anyone who has faced the unimaginable and wondered how to move forward. It is for those who are trapped in the weight of resentment and longing for freedom.

Forgiveness is not the end of the story—it is the beginning of redemption. As you read these pages, I pray you'll find hope, healing, and the courage to choose love over hate, faith over fear, and forgiveness over anger.

Welcome to this journey. You are not alone.

CHAPTER ONE

THE JOURNEY THAT PREPARED ME

"God gives you a story to give Him the glory."
—Apostle Fred L. Hodge, Jr.

My life has many chapters. I believe every chapter has led me to this moment. My pastor, Apostle Fred L. Hodge, once shared a quote during a Sunday service, *"God gives you a story to give Him the glory,"* and it resonated deeply with me. My story, though marked by pain and struggle, is ultimately about God's glory—about how He carried me through life's trials and shaped me into the person I am today.

My life's story began with a profound loss: my mother passed away when I was just three years old. By the time I was five, I had faced more pain than most adults. I was struck by a truck, breaking both legs and crushing my pelvis, leaving me in a body cast for over a year. From there, life became a series of upheavals.

I lived in eleven different homes by the age of fifteen, moving between my father's girlfriends, some of whom inflicted overwhelming abuse. One tried to strangle me. Another beat me with an extension cord, embedding pins into my skin, then forced me to bathe, amplifying the pain. A stepbrother once gave me food and then taunted me, claiming it was poisoned.

Such experiences left me fearful and timid, afraid to speak up for myself. Fear wasn't just an emotion—it became a shadow over my life. Amid this chaos, God's hand was at work. At fifteen, I moved in with my great-aunt, a Missionary in the Pentecostal church. For the first time, I was introduced to a stable, faith-filled environment. It was there I accepted Christ as my Savior and began seeking a deeper relationship with Him.

However, challenges persisted. After high school, I moved to Los Angeles, trying to escape my past. God intervened again, placing me in the care of a pastor's family until I married in 1982. My marriage became a new chapter of healing and growth. Together, my husband and I built a life centered on faith and raised four children—three daughters and one son.

Looking back, I see how God used my struggles to strengthen me for the path ahead. He shielded me from relationships that could have led to further harm and surrounded me with people who nurtured my faith. Every step prepared me for the most challenging chapter of my life: the loss of my son, Charles.

Life hasn't been easy, but through every trial, God has shown me that my story is not about pain—it's about purpose. It's about His glory and the transformative power of His love.

CHAPTER TWO

OUR SON

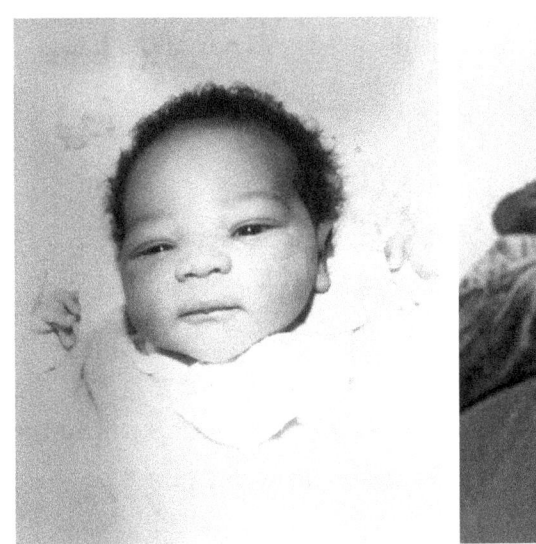 

Charles Emmanuel Briggs

Charles Emmanuel Briggs was born on December 19, 1986, and his life was tragically cut short on August 23, 2014. For 27 years, God blessed us with a son whose love, laughter, and unwavering compassion touched everyone around him.

UNDENIABLY GUILTY, POSITIVELY FORGIVEN

From the moment Charles entered our lives, he brought joy and a sense of completeness to our family. As the only boy among three sisters—Charlena, Charlynnae, and Charmaine—Charles took his role as the "man of the house" very seriously, even though his father was always present. He was fiercely protective, often stepping in like a second father and guardian.

I remember one morning when one of his sisters was heading out for school, her face all made up like she was ready for a photo shoot. Charles turned to me, eyebrows raised, and said, "Mom, are you going to let her go to school looking like that?" That was Charles—always watching out for his sisters, always the protective big brother.

He loved his three sisters; and he longed for a brother. After my last daughter was born, Charles said, "Mom, you promised me a brother." I reminded him that if he were to have a brother at his age, he would be upset with him for being in his room, messing with his model cars and trucks. Fortunately, that ended that conversation because Charles never mentioned having a brother again.

Charles' compassion was boundless, and his charisma drew people to him. From an early age, he showed an extraordinary awareness of others' needs. One day, while he was in elementary school, he asked me to pack an extra lunch. When I asked why, he simply said, "There's a kid at school who doesn't have anything to eat, and I want to share with him." Moments like these were not rare—they were the norm with Charles.

Another time, while we were getting out of the car at the grocery store, Charles spotted an elderly man smoking nearby. Without hesitation, he approached the man and said, "If you don't stop smoking, you're going to die." Embarrassed, I tried to pull Charles away, but to my surprise, the man nodded solemnly and replied, "I know, son. I wish I could stop." Charles' honesty was fearless, but it was always rooted in genuine concern for others.

He had also had a gift for turning strangers into family. Since he didn't have a biological brother. Charles created his own—building friendships that crossed cultural and ethnic boundaries. His ability to forge deep connections left a lasting legacy of love and loyalty.

Raised in a Christian home, Charles held steadfast to the values we taught him, including respect for women and a commitment to forgiveness. On the night he was murdered, his concern was for a young woman he did not even know.

Charles' humor was infectious, and he had a gift for making people laugh. One of my favorite memories is from his time at WyoTech in Wyoming, where he studied auto mechanics.

After Charles' graduation, we helped clean the house he shared with his roommates. As I tidied up his room, I noticed a pile of linens on the floor. Behind me, I heard Charles say, "Watch my Mom." When I bent down to pick up the linen, I jumped back in shock—there was fake dog poop hidden underneath the linen! Charles and his friends burst into laughter hysterically. Even now, the silly little prop is one of my most cherished keepsakes. It reminds me of his playful spirit and how Charles could turn the most mundane moments into something special.

Another cherished memory is the time Charles and I were cooking chicken together. As we worked, he suddenly said, "Mom, we need some rosemary." When I told him we didn't have any, he paused for a moment, then smiled and said, "Oh, landscapers use it all the time." Without missing a beat, he went outside, found some rosemary, brought it back, washed it, and we used it in our dish.

Charles's life was a testament to love in action. Whether helping a runaway find her way home or standing up for someone in need, he lived by the values we instilled in him. At times, I questioned whether we had done something wrong in raising him—why did Charles always feel the need to defend and protect others? But now, I see it differently. His actions reflected God's love working through him.

Though Charles is no longer with us, his legacy lives on in the countless lives he touched. His friends still call and visit, sharing stories of how he changed their lives. His sisters remember him as their guardian, their confidant, and their biggest cheerleader.

> *"A merry heart doeth good like a medicine: but a broken spirit drieth the bones."*
>
> Proverbs 17:22 (KJV)

Charles was more than a son—he was a gift. His laughter was a balm to the soul, his compassion a light in dark times, and his forgiveness a reminder of God's unending grace. His story doesn't end with his death; it continues in the love he left behind and the lessons he taught us about living with purpose and faith.

My son was not perfect, but one thing is for sure: he loved God. Many nights, he would ask me to pray with him. Sometimes, he would ask me about a scripture that maybe he wanted to give to his friends. As I stated above, I prayed many nights for my son, just like I pray for my family to be saved and to know Jesus Christ as their Lord and Savior. There is no doubt in my mind that Charles was able to repent and ask for forgiveness at the time of his death. Somewhere between being picked up by the paramedics to surgery and recovery. He repented and asked for forgiveness.

Knowing my son, I truly believe that if he were here today, he would forgive Garrett. That's just who Charles was—always choosing love and reconciliation over anger and bitterness.

CHAPTER THREE

FORGIVENESS WAS A NECESSITY

When I first learned of my son Charles' murder, it felt as though my world had come to an end. Grief consumed me, but it wasn't just the loss that shattered us—it was the manner of his death and the racial tension surrounding it.

The weapon used to kill Charles was a compound bow and hunting arrow designed for large animal hunting. Garrett knew exactly what he was doing; he was skilled in hunting from a young age. After the act, he used the "N" word to describe what he had done, intensifying our pain with the sting of racism.

Murder is cruel and sudden. It robs you of the chance to say goodbye. Unlike the gradual acceptance that can come with illness, this kind of loss is abrupt and beyond comprehension. Twenty-four hours passed before we even knew Charles was gone.

He had no ID on him, so his body was taken to the Los Angeles County Morgue for identification. The pain of waiting, of not knowing, is indescribable.

Parents expect to be buried by their children—not the other way around. Nothing prepares you for burying your child.

FAITH AS A FOUNDATION

In the face of such unfathomable grief, my faith became my refuge. I leaned heavily on scripture, especially Ephesians 4:26 (KJV),

> *"Be ye angry, and sin not: let not the sun go down upon your wrath."*

These words validated my anger while reminding me not to let it control me.

Another verse that carried me through was Romans 12:19 (KJV),

> *"Vengeance is mine: I will repay, said the Lord."*

In those early days, I clung to the promise that justice was not mine to enact. My heart wanted retribution, but I knew that vengeance belongs to God.

THE JOURNEY TO FORGIVENESS

Forgiveness did not come easily or quickly. It was a deliberate, intentional journey, one that required prayer and surrender. Here are the steps I took:

1. **Giving Thanks:** I held fast to 1 Thessalonians 5:18 (KJV),
   "In everything give thanks: for this is the will of God in Christ Jesus concerning you."
   Every time the thought of Charles' murder came to mind, I would tell God, "I don't understand this, but I thank you anyway."

2. **Praying for Garrett and his Family:** It wasn't easy to pray for the man who murdered my son, but I knew it was necessary.

3. **Choosing Action Over Despair:** Grief threatened to paralyze me, but I refused to let it. I got out of bed each morning, went about my daily routine, and stayed busy.

Some days, it feels manageable; other days, it feels insurmountable. I made a decision early on not to let grief consume me. I'd seen others lose themselves in sorrow, and I did not want that for my life.

LIVING WITH GRIEF

Grief is a long journey, one that doesn't end with the passing of time. There is a sisterhood among mothers who have lost children to murder—a shared understanding that binds us.

Years before Charles was taken from us, I met a mother whose son had been tragically murdered many years earlier. I remember the countless times she shared her story with me, recounting her pain and how God had carried her through such a devastating experience. Looking back now, I realize that God placed her in my life to prepare me for the loss of my son. When my tragedy struck, she became an unwavering source of strength and encouragement, guiding me through the darkest moments of my life.

Through this experience, I've learned that grief cannot be rushed. It's different for everyone and it comes in waves. A song, a scent, or a memory can bring it back in an instant. It's important to allow yourself to feel, to cry, and to remember.

I remember reading *Experiencing Grief,* by C. Norman Wright, a book that was recommended to me early in my grieving process. Wright shared that even decades after his own loss, grief still ambushed him from time to time. That insight was liberating—it gave me permission to grieve without guilt, no matter how much time had passed.

HOW GRIEF CHANGED ME

Grief doesn't just bring sorrow—it transforms you. It shapes you in ways you never expected, sometimes giving you the strength to fight battles you never thought you'd have to face.

> *"Sorrow is better than laughter: for by the sadness of the countenance the heart is made better."*
>
> Ecclesiastes 7:3 (KJV)

I once read an article in *O, The Oprah Magazine* titled *The Flipside of Grief.* It explored how, despite the deep pain of loss, some people emerge from grief changed for the better. I've always considered myself to be a good person, but when my son was murdered, something in me changed.

I can't fully explain it—perhaps one day God will reveal it to me—but something inside me shifted in a way that was noticeable to those who knew me. Even now, I struggle to comprehend exactly what took place within me. Psychologists write about the ways trauma reshapes a person, but all I know for certain is that my grief gave me **the fortitude to fight for justice for my son**.

It took three years before we finally went to trial. Just two weeks before the trial was set to begin, I received a call from the District Attorney who had worked with us for those three years. He told me he was being transferred to Los Angeles and would no longer be handling our case. I was **infuriated**. This DA had bonded with my family, had stood with us through the most painful years of our lives. The thought of losing him just before the trial felt like another devastating blow.

But something in me refused to accept it.

Before Charles' death, I don't know if I would have had the tenacity to fight the way I did. But grief changed me. I began making phone calls, arranging meetings. I met with the **head deputy at the courthouse**, then with the **attorneys assigned to replace our DA**. I told them, *"No reflection on you, I know you're highly skilled with excellent trial records, but I want our DA to remain on this case."*

I didn't stop there. I **reached out to the Los Angeles County District Attorney's office** and formally requested that our DA not be removed. I wasn't willing to let someone who had walked with us for three years be taken from us just before the trial began.

And in the end, **I accomplished my goal**. The DA remained on our case.

The bond we formed with him continues to this day.

Before Charles' death, I wouldn't have imagined myself standing in front of attorneys, making demands, pushing for justice with such determination. But grief made me stronger in ways I never anticipated. It didn't break me—it pushed me forward.

SEEKING JUSTICE

Three years after Charles' murder, Garrett Adams was sentenced to 25 years to life for first-degree felony murder with mayhem, with an additional year for using the bow and arrow. But our journey didn't end there.

Six years later, Garrett won an appeal due to a technical error in how the judge explained mayhem to the jury. We were forced to go through a second trial. The process reopened old wounds for my family—my daughters, my husband, and myself. We were apprehensive about working with a new district attorney, but over time, those fears eased.

Through it all, I held onto a word God placed in my spirit: equitable. I looked it up and found its root word, equity, which means "fair and just." That promise sustained me, reminding me that God's justice would prevail.

Nearly eight years after Charles' murder, I began exchanging letters with Garret. It's a relationship I never imagined possible, but God has worked in ways I cannot fully explain. You will see excerpts throughout this book, showing how forgiveness and healing can transcend even the greatest pain.

I want to speak directly to mothers who have lost children: Grief is a journey, and it's different for everyone. Don't let anyone tell you how or when to move on. You carried that child close to your heart, and their absence will always leave an ache. But don't let grief overwhelm your life.

Memories are a gift. Cherish them. In time, you will laugh again, and the memories will bring joy rather than just pain. Choose to live, to remember, and to honor your child's life through your own.

JOURNEY OF FORGIVENESS AND HEALING

"And whenever you stand praying, forgive, if you have anything against anyone, so that your Father also who is in heaven may forgive you your trespasses."

Mark 11:25

REFLECTION:

Forgiveness is not easy, but it is necessary. Holding onto anger and bitterness only weighs us down, preventing us from experiencing God's peace. When we forgive, we reflect God's love and open ourselves to healing. It doesn't mean we excuse the wrong, but rather, we choose to let go and trust God to bring justice in His time.

PRAYER:

"Lord, I struggle with letting go of my pain, but I know You call me to forgive. Please soften my heart and help me to release my anger into Your hands. I trust You to heal what is broken. Amen."

CHAPTER FOUR

THE KNOCK ON
THE DOOR

Saturday started like any other. The warm aroma of marinara filled our home as I prepared one of Charles' favorite meals—meatball subs. I glanced at the clock, anticipating the sound of the front door opening, the sight of his familiar smile, and his, "Hey, Mom, what smells so good?" But as the hours stretched into the evening, worry crept in. His phone went straight to voicemail. Midnight came and went, and still, no sign of him.

Before Charles was murdered, I prayed fervently for my son to be saved. I'm not suggesting that God took him to answer my prayers. Yet, the scripture says in Proverbs 18:10 (KJV),

> *"The name of the Lord is a strong tower; the righteous run into it and are safe."*

Repeatedly that scripture came to my spirit, a divine whisper of assurance that I did not fully understand at the time.

Charles lived with us, though it was not unusual for him to stay out. I did not think much of his absence as I prepared my sermon to speak at church. My pastor was out of town, and I wanted to ensure my message was ready. Around 1:00 a.m., I heard noises at the door. It sounded as though someone was trying to get in. Assuming it was Charles, I looked out the kitchen window, but Charles wasn't there. Relieved but uneasy, I went back to bed.

As I lay down, a voice in my spirit interrupted the stillness: *They are going to come to the door about Charles.* It wasn't panic but a deep, unsettling certainty that gripped me. Within twenty minutes, the doorbell rang. When I peered out, two detectives stood at the door, somber and unyielding. If you've ever had detectives come to your door, you know—they don't bring good news.

Without thinking, I opened the door but refused to hear them, "I do not want to hear anything you have to say," I blurted out and retreated into the house, leaving them standing outside.

My husband stepped forward to speak with them as I hovered in the bedroom, too terrified to face the truth. A few moments later, I returned to stand beside my husband. Their words shattered our world: Charles had been murdered—with a hunting bow and arrow by a friend, Garrett Adams. The name was unfamiliar to us because we knew most of our son's friends.

I had to call our three daughters, Charlena, Charlynnae, and Charmaine and tell them the unthinkable. Numb with grief, I struggled to process that my son, my Charles, was gone.

THE NEXT MORNING

The next morning, our family went to church together. The Lord gave me the strength to speak, and a soul came to Christ that day. Despite the weight of sorrow, I felt God's power, and His anointing was upon me in a mighty way.

You might wonder how I managed it. The answer lies in the scripture, particularly 2 Corinthians 12:9 (KJV):

> *"My grace is sufficient for you, for My strength is made perfect in our weakness."*

At my lowest, His strength sustained me. My former pastor, Bishop E.E. Cleveland, Sr., often quoted 2 Chronicles 16:9a (KJV)

> *"For the eyes of the Lord run to and fro throughout the whole earth, to show Himself strong on behalf of those whose heart is loyal to Him. "*

In moments of despair, these truths anchored me. Through the fog of grief, I clung to His promises, renewing my mind with His Word daily.

UNDENIABLY GUILTY, POSITIVELY FORGIVEN

Isaiah 55:8-9 says,

"For my thoughts are not your thoughts, neither are your ways my ways, saith the Lord. For as the heavens are higher than the earth, so are my ways higher than your ways, and my thoughts than your thoughts." (KJV)

We don't think like God does, and that's why it's essential for us to have the mind of Christ. Our finite human minds can only grasps so much, and it is through the renewing our minds with His Word that we align with His eternal perspective.

"He Was There All the Time" are the words to a song I heard many years ago. "He was there all the time, waiting patiently in line. He was there all the time." One day, I was looking back over the facts of my son's murder. As I was thinking and meditating, I thought about how, even in death, God was there with Charles.

There were so many things that had transpired during his demise that caused me to believe and feel in my spirit, and even though I didn't quite understand, I realized that even in death, God is there because it's His desire that none would perish but that all would come to know Him. Another scripture came to mind, Romans 10:13, which says,

"For whosoever shall call upon the name of the Lord shall be saved." (KJV)

As I recall the events of that night, I was told that Charles could be heard as he was running and calling on God.

I didn't find out some things until the first trial; three years later, I found out that the night Charles was murdered he was trying to run home. A registered nurse testified he happened to be driving in the neighborhood and saw Charles approach him and collapse. The nurse stated Charles had a "penetrating chest wound" and was bleeding profusely. The nurse rendered aid until the police arrived. The nurse, also a recreational hunter, said the arrow, which was sticking out of Charles' back, had a "broad head" tip used by hunters.

I was then confident, that God had orchestrated that moment, and even though I didn't clearly understand everything, I could see God's hand, even in the death of my son in that tragic situation; God was there.

We live and operate in time; God operates in eternity. The trauma nurse was a hunter and familiar with bows and arrows. He also relayed information to the trauma team about the extent of Charles' injuries to prepare the team when Charles arrived at the hospital. Only God could have set the situation up for the trauma nurse to be there at the right time.

I have always been the mother concerned about who kept my children, who they knew, and who they were with. So, it was settling for me to know that God had orchestrated that a trauma nurse would be there when he needed to be. So, I thank God. As I keep mentioning, I don't understand it all, but I know God was there in the midst of the entire situation. He was there with our son.

One of Charles' brothers, Lawrence, visited us the night before the funeral. He had just flown in from another country, where he played basketball. As we were sitting on the couch talking, I was going to say something to Lawrence; I felt the words coming from the pit of my stomach. I opened my mouth, and the scripture came out, *"Absent from the body, present with the Lord."* 2 Corinthians 5:8 (KJV) That was not what I was planning to say. At that moment, God gave me peace the night before the funeral that Charles was with Him. Ultimately, we want to know when our loved ones transition; we want peace in knowing they are with the Lord, I thank God for letting me know He was there all the time. God has promised in His word to be with us. One scripture says,

Low, I'm with you always, even to the end of the age.
                                        Matthew 28:20 (NKJV)

It's one of my favorite scripture.

SURRENDERING THE PAIN

"He heals the brokenhearted and binds up their wounds."

Psalm 147:3

REFLECTION:

When we experience deep loss and betrayal, the pain can feel unbearable. But God does not leave us in our suffering. He sees every tear and promises to heal our wounds. The first step is surrender—giving our pain to Him, knowing that He is the ultimate Healer.

PRAYER:

"Father, my heart is heavy, and I struggle to carry this burden. Help me to trust You with my pain. Heal my heart and remind me that You are near to the brokenhearted. Amen."

CHAPTER FIVE

THE FIRST TRIAL

The details of his murder came in fragments over the next few days. Garrett Adams, a young man we didn't know, had murdered Charles with a compound bow and arrow—a weapon designed to hunt game, not humans. The absurdity of it made the pain sharper. Who uses a hunting bow on another person?

But Garrett didn't stop at murder. He and his accomplices wove a story of lies to justify their actions. They claimed Charles had broken into their home and that he was the aggressor. Those lies were like a second death, staining the memory of a young man who deserved so much better.

The trial was a blur of grief and resolve. I sat in that courtroom, gripping a small cross, whispering prayers. "Lord, let Your truth prevail." The defense painted a picture of Charles that wasn't my son. They claimed he was violent and that he had fought Garrett and caused his injuries. But they lied!

UNDENIABLY GUILTY, POSITIVELY FORGIVEN

God's truth is unstoppable.

The turning point came when Garrett's girlfriend, who had initially supported his story, took the stand. Her voice trembled as she admitted the truth: *"Charles didn't break into our house. Garrett attacked him."* Her words cracked the carefully constructed lies wide open. The defense's case unraveled like a frayed thread.

Even Garrett's supposed injuries—a scratched retina—were revealed to be self-inflicted. He had walked into a tree branch. The truth stood, naked, and undeniable, while the lies crumbled under its weight.

I thought of an old story my former pastor would tell about *Lie* and *Truth* going swimming. *Lie* got out of the water and stole *Truth's* clothes, parading through town, pretending to be something it wasn't. But eventually, *Truth* emerged, bare and undeniable. That day in court, I saw *Truth* walk tall and victorious.

Garrett was convicted of first-degree felony murder and sentenced to 25 years to life, with a one-year enhancement for using a weapon classified as a razor. While the verdict brought some relief, it wasn't enough. How could such a barbaric weapon carry only a single-year enhancement?

During the first trial, an archery expert testified about the mechanics of a **compound bow**, the weapon that took Charles' life. The expert explained that compound bows are commonly used for hunting and target practice because they allow an archer to "hold on target a little longer," making them highly accurate. He described how the cams on the bow create a "let-off" point, where after a certain amount of force is applied, the bow reduces the pressure, allowing for greater precision.

The expert identified the arrow Garrett used as a **broadhead hunting arrow**, razor-sharp and specifically designed for hunting **large game** such as deer and elk. These arrows were meant to **pierce major blood vessels, the heart, or the lungs**, ensuring that the animal "bleeds out quickly."

The prosecution wanted the jury to understand the significance of this weapon—**this was not a mistake. This was not an accident. The weapon Garrett used was designed to kill**.

Determined to make a change, I partnered with my local Assemblyman to draft legislation increasing penalties for crimes committed with unconventional weapons like the arrow that was used to murder Charles. We fought hard, gathering stories and statistics, but the bill fell one vote short of reaching the Senate floor. That loss stung, but it wasn't the end. Charles' story would continue to fuel my fight.

Through it all, I leaned on my faith. When despair threatened to consume me, I turned to God's Word.

"And ye shall know the truth, and the truth shall make you free."
John 8:32 (KJV)

Those words became my anchor. The lies spoken about my son didn't have the final say. God's truth prevailed in the courtroom, just as it always does.

RACISM AND JUSTICE

Racism didn't just kill my son; it silenced his story, erasing the deeper truth of what happened that night. But I won't let it win. Charles' life mattered, and his legacy will shine through the darkness.

Every day, I carry Charles in my heart. His laugh, his smile, the way he always offered to help others—those memories fuel me. Garrett took my son's life, but Charles' story isn't over. I fought for laws protecting others, a world where lies can't obscure the truth, and a society where every life is valued.

Charles taught me to love fiercely and to stand boldly for what's right. His legacy is one of justice, truth, and unwavering faith, and I'll honor it as long as I live.

Our son's murder was the second bow and arrow murder in the Antelope Valley where we live. The Antelope Valley is located in northern **Los Angeles County** and the southeastern portion of **Kern County**, California. I pray that one day, the Senate will pass a bill to increase the enhancements on such a weapon.

I understand hunters favor the compound bow and arrow for hunting, and my problem was not with hunters having access and using the bow and arrow for hunting purposes. My problem is when you take a human life with a hunting bow and arrow, there should be steeper consequences for the enhancement should have been greater. Unfortunately, human life does not mean much anymore in this day and age.

Thank God for the truth! During the trial, as I have mentioned, many lies were told, and they started the night of the murder. Garrett's paternal twin brother, and Garrett's girlfriend, who Garrett had beaten up, came up with this story to cover up the murder.

But you know God is a Spirit, and His Word is true. He said that we would know the truth, and the truth will make us free or set us free, and I tell you, even though lies were told, the truth came out at the very beginning. The truth came out when Garrett's girlfriend testified. What she said on the witness stand was not what she told the night it happened.

They had all decided to say that Charles had broken into their house.

But God allowed the truth to come forth. I'm saying that the truth will always win because Jesus is the Truth. He is the truth, and during the trial, our prayer was, "Let your truth prevail because you are the Spirit of Truth."

In my experience, and that of others, the Antelope Valley has long carried an undertone of racial tension. This belief was solidified when my son, at 17, was assaulted by a Caucasian man, and despite reporting the incident, no action was taken. Tragically, his later murder further underscored these concerns, as the facts and the use of a racial slur strongly suggested a hate crime. However, the District Attorney declined to pursue that charge, citing the difficulty of proving intent, opting instead to focus on a 1st-degree murder case, which they felt confident they could win.

So it made us feel that we wouldn't receive justice in our case because of everything that was going on, but we couldn't continue looking negatively at the situation. The one thing we had to do was stand on, or I had to stand on, what God had told me. God had told me He was just, and I believed that, and I stood on it.

An appeal was granted due to a judicial error. The term mayhem in the judicial realm means to maim and not kill.

However, when you engage a compound bow with six razor-sharp blades, the intent is to kill in my mind. But unfortunately, because of that error, we had to go back to trial.

WEAPONS USED IN THE CASE OF CHARLES EMMANUEL BRIGGS

For readers unfamiliar with compound bows and broadhead hunting arrows, the following diagrams illustrate the weapons involved in this case. These images are included to provide context for the court testimony and the severity of the injuries inflicted.

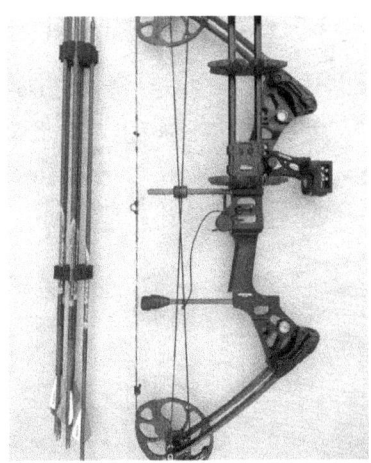

The Compound Bow

A compound bow, like the one Garrett Adams used, is a powerful hunting weapon designed for accuracy. The "let-off" feature allows an archer to hold their shot longer while using less effort, making the bow more precise and deadly. These bows are commonly used to hunt large animals, including deer, black bears, and even moose.

The Broadhead Hunting Arrow

Broadhead hunting arrows are designed to inflict deep, lethal wounds. The razor-sharp blades expand upon impact, ensuring that the target suffers massive blood loss and organ damage. These arrows are commonly used by hunters aiming for major organs such as the heart or lungs to ensure a swift kill.

STRENGTH IN WEAKNESS

"My grace is sufficient for you, for my power is made perfect in weakness."

2 Corinthians 12:9

REFLECTION:

Forgiving someone who has hurt us deeply may feel impossible. But God never asks us to do it alone. His grace gives us the strength to do what we cannot do in our own power. When we feel weak, we can lean on Him, knowing He will carry us through.

PRAYER:

"Lord, I don't feel strong enough to forgive, but I know Your grace is enough. Give me the strength I need to take the next step in my healing journey. Amen."

CHAPTER SIX

THE RETRIAL

Seven years after Charles' murder, we were back in court for a retrial due to an appeal. This time, I faced the process with the lessons God had taught me in the years prior. But the weight of uncertainty still loomed.

The retrial began on the same day as the trial for the murder of Ahmaud Arbery—a young Black man who was murdered during a racially motivated hate crime while jogging in Satilla Shores, a neighborhood near Brunswick in Glynn County, Georgia. It was a sobering reminder of the racial tensions that still plague our society.

From the moment I walked into the courtroom, doubt tried to creep in. The jury didn't seem favorable, and the circumstances felt overwhelming. Negative voices told me we might lose this time, but I held onto God's promises.

And, I had to hold onto my faith. I was told by someone I looked up to as the second trial was approaching that things might be different this time. I had to recall what God had spoken to me the first time. You see, God does not change. The scripture says,

For I am the Lord, I change not;

Malachi 3:6 (KJV)

My family, friends, and I were consistently praying during the retrial. As the defense attorney was preparing to present his final argument to the jury, he appeared shaken, struggling to regain his composure. At one point, he couldn't even gather his thoughts. It reminded me of a story in 2 Chronicles 20:20-24, where God confused the enemies of Judah, leading to their defeat. In that courtroom, I witnessed God's power at work.

By the time of the second trial, the prosecution brought in another archery expert—this time a deputy with extensive experience handling hunting weapons. This expert confirmed what the other archery expert had said in the first trial. He explained that Garrett's **compound bow** was not just a basic archery tool but a weapon for **hunting large animals, including deer, black bears,** and **even moose.** It was **equipped with razor-tip hunting arrows, each over an inch in diameter,** meant to create a large wound, ensuring that the target "bled out quickly."

The deputy **test-fired Adams' bow**, confirming its accuracy. After **reviewing surveillance footage of the shooting**, he testified that Adams **had fully drawn the bow before releasing the arrow**, which meant that the shot was **deliberate and intentional**. The conclusion was undeniable:

This was no accident. This was an execution.

God is the same yesterday, today, and forever more. So I had to retrieve the Word God spoke to me seven years ago and hold on to it - regardless of the negative things around me. When faced with difficulty, we must seek God and have an ear to hear Him. We must choose to stand firm on what He has already spoken to us even though people are saying something else. We cannot look at the circumstances.

Believe me when I say this: When Garrett told his attorney that he wanted to address the court, we did not know what he would say or expect. During the first trial, he was silent. But in this trial, Garrett stood up, looked at our family, and said, *"I am so sorry for what I've done. There is not a day that goes by that I don't think about Charles."* He then asked for forgiveness.

Oh my God, my daughters' response echoed throughout the Courtroom. They sounded like they were speaking into a microphone as they both said in unison, "I Forgive You!"

Their words rippled through the courtroom with a power that felt almost heavenly. I cannot explain to this day, only to say that God manifested in that Courtroom in a way that touched the hearts of the people there. Observers later told me people in the room were crying, wiping their eyes.

Walking out of the Courtroom that day, I was overwhelmed by the peace that forgiveness had brought. The power of God's love and grace had touched not only our hearts but also those of everyone present.

CHAPTER SEVEN

AFTER THE VERDICT— MY JOURNEY BEYOND THE COURTROOM

When tragedy strikes, the road to justice can be long and painful. My family and I experienced this firsthand as we endured not just one, but two trials in the wake of my son's murder. The courtroom became both a battleground and a place where I wrestled with emotions I never thought I'd have to face—anger, grief, frustration, and eventually, forgiveness.

In this chapter, I have chosen to include key court documents and trial excerpts that detail the events surrounding Charles' death and the legal proceedings that followed. These records serve as more than just legal evidence; they are a testament to the weight of what was lost and the pursuit of justice that came after.

Reading these words on paper does not compare to the heartache of sitting in that courtroom, hearing every painful detail spoken aloud. I remember the weight of each testimony, the emotions that flooded me as I watched the proceedings unfold, and the reality that no sentence, no verdict, could ever bring my son back. But through it all, I also found moments of clarity—an understanding that justice on earth is imperfect, but God's justice is unfailing.

Following the documents, I will share my personal reflections on both trials, the emotions I carried through each phase, and the moment I realized that forgiveness was the only way forward.

COURT OF APPEAL OF THE STATE OF CALIFORNIA SECOND APPELLATE DISTRICT DIVISION SEVEN

People v. Adams

INTRODUCTION

Garrett Taylor Adams (Adams) appeals from the judgment entered after a jury acquitted him of first degree premeditated murder but convicted him of first degree mayhem felony murder and found he personally used a deadly or dangerous weapon. Adams argues, among other things, that substantial evidence did not support the jury's finding he specifically intended to commit mayhem and that the trial court's instruction on mayhem felony murder was erroneous. We conclude that there was substantial evidence Adams specifically intended to commit mayhem, but that the trial court prejudicially erred when it instructed the jury on the specific intent element of mayhem felony murder. Therefore, we reverse.

FACTUAL AND PROCEDURAL BACKGROUND

Adams Shoots Briggs with a Compound Bow and Kills Him. Adams was an experienced, licensed hunter. He had not purchased meat in a store in over seven years. He hunted deer and other game with a rifle and with a compound bow, which is a bow that uses a wheel and pulley system that allows it to be drawn and held at different "draw weights." Adams knew never to point a weapon at anything he did not intend to shoot. One evening Adams was drinking alcohol with his girlfriend, at their home in Lancaster. Adams got into a physical altercation with his girlfriend, and went to a local bar. When he returned at 3:00 a.m., he fought again with her. Adams's twin brother, and friend, Charles Briggs, arrived and got into an argument with Adams. All three men were drunk. The physical altercation between Adams and his girlfriend evolved into a fight among Adams, his brother, and Briggs. The three men wrestled and threw punches at each other, and there was "a lot of yelling." The fight eventually stopped, and Adams went inside the house, leaving his brother and Briggs in the driveway. Adam's brother and Briggs argued and shoved each other. Adams emerged from the house some minutes later with his compound bow and several razor-tip hunting arrows. Adams stood still for a moment before Briggs noticed him with the bow. Briggs said, "What, are you going to shoot me?" Adams told Briggs, "You'd better leave, or I'll shoot you." Briggs, who was angry and yelling, dared Adams to shoot him. He said, "What do you think? I'm scared to die? Shoot it. Just let it go." Adams, who was "very, very angry" and "puffing his chest," walked toward Briggs as Briggs backed away. The distance between Adams and Briggs decreased to several feet and then increased to 20 feet. Adams told his brother to move because he was blocking Adams's shot. Briggs raised his arms away from his body at the elbows and turned his palms up. Adams raised the bow, drew it, aimed at Briggs, and without hesitating fired an arrow. Briggs hunched over and stepped back saying, "Oh, my God, why'd you do that?" Adams said, "I shot that nigger," "That's what you get, homie," and "I should shoot you with my gun, homie, you better run." (Investigating officers subsequently found a rifle and a loaded magazine in Adams's house.) Adams also stated, "When I tell you I'm going to shoot you, you better run."

The arrow entered Briggs's right upper chest, traveled downward, and protruded out his back. The arrow pierced Briggs's diaphragm, lacerated his liver and pancreas, and ruptured his spleen. Briggs walked down the street before collapsing. A registered nurse happened to see Briggs fall and rendered aid until paramedics arrived. Briggs died during emergency surgery.

Adams Makes Up a Story About What Happened

After Adams shot Briggs, he handed the bow to his girlfriend, and told her to put it "somewhere" and call 911. Adams went to a neighbor's house, pounded on the door, said "that nigger got in my house," and asked the neighbor to call the police. Adams told his girlfriend to "stick to the story and say that someone broke in our house and he had shot [him]." In a telephone call made and recorded while Adams was in custody, Adams asked an unidentified listener to tell his girlfriend "to keep her mouth shut . . . cause that's crucial for me." He added, "Make sure . . . when you see her, tell her make sure she's not out there flapping her lips about this shit. . . ."

The People's Archery Expert Testifies
the Shooting Was Not an Accident.

The prosecution's archery expert, testified that Adams's compound bow was for hunting large game such as deer, black bear, elk, and, at close range, moose. The bow was equipped to use razor-tip hunting arrows that measured more than an inch in diameter. The arrows were designed to create a large wound that would cause an animal to bleed out quickly, with the goal of killing the animal "quickly and humanely."

The deputy test-fired Adams's bow and concluded it was fairly accurate. In the Deputy's opinion, Adams had fully drawn the bow before he fired the arrow at Briggs. The Deputy viewed a video of the shooting and concluded it was not an accident.

The Jury Convicts Adams

The jury acquitted Adams of first degree premeditated murder, but convicted him of first degree mayhem felony murder (Pen. Code, §§ 187, subd. (a), 189). The jury also found Adams personally used a deadly or dangerous weapon (§ 12022, subd. (b)(1)). The trial court sentenced Adams to a prison term of 25 years to life for first degree mayhem felony murder plus one year for the deadly or dangerous weapon enhancement.

I never imagined I would sit in a courtroom, waiting to hear the fate of the man who took my son's life. As the verdict was read, time seemed to stop. My heart pounded, my hands trembled, and I held my breath, unsure of what I wanted to hear. Justice? Yes. But would justice ever be enough?

THE MOMENT THE VERDICT WAS READ

When the words "Guilty" were spoken, a wave of emotions crashed over me—relief, sadness, anger, exhaustion. I had prayed for this moment, yet I still felt empty. A guilty verdict didn't bring my son back. A prison sentence didn't erase my grief. There was no ruling that could restore what was lost.

As I looked at Garrett Adams, I wondered if he felt any remorse. Did he truly understand what he had done? Did he regret it? Or was he simply resigned to his punishment? My mind raced with questions that I knew would never be answered.

DID JUSTICE FEEL SUFFICIENT?

People told me that this verdict was justice, but justice felt incomplete. The legal system had done its part, but my heart was still heavy. In that moment, I realized that true justice—God's justice—was far greater than anything that could be handed down by a judge. No human ruling could bring peace to my heart. Only God could.

After the trial ended, many people asked me, "Do you feel better now?" My answer was complicated. I was grateful for accountability, but justice alone didn't heal the wounds in my heart. There was still a deeper battle to fight—the battle for peace, for healing, for forgiveness.

PROCESSING MY FAITH IN THE AFTERMATH

Leaving the courtroom, I knew I had a choice. I could let bitterness consume me, or I could take steps toward healing. I thought about Jesus on the cross, whispering

> *"Father, forgive them, for they know not what they do."*
>
> Luke 23:34

If Jesus could forgive the very people who crucified Him, could I forgive the man who took my son's life?

I won't lie—my first answer was no. How could I forgive someone who had caused so much pain? I wrestled with God over this question. But the more I prayed, the clearer it became: forgiveness wasn't about letting Garrett go free. It was about freeing myself from the weight of anger and grief.

THE SECOND TRIAL - A DIFFERENT KIND OF BATTLE

Sitting through a second trial was even harder than the first. By then, I had already endured months of grief, sleepless nights, and moments where my faith felt like it was hanging by a thread. Reliving the details of Charles' death again was excruciating, but something had changed in me.

By the second trial, I wasn't just looking for a guilty verdict—I was looking for peace. I was desperate for a way to move forward, to reclaim my life, and to break free from the pain that had consumed me since that tragic day.

Of all the painful moments I experienced in the courtroom, **one of the most hurtful was hearing my son compared to a bear.**

I remember that day so clearly—the way those words cut through me, the way I felt my breath leave my body. **Someone in the courtroom, without hesitation or shame, compared Charles' life to that of a bear.**

The moment I heard it, I felt like I couldn't breathe. The weight of that statement hit me like a blow, as if my son's life—his hopes, his dreams, his entire existence—had been reduced to nothing more than a **hunting target**. I couldn't sit there any longer. I left the courtroom in tears, stepping outside, **overcome with emotion.**

The person who spoke those words showed **no empathy, no compassion** for our family. They spoke as if my son's life was disposable, as if his death was nothing more than a hunting accident. But Charles wasn't an animal—**he was my son**.

According to the coroner's report, Charles' liver was perforated, his pancreas was lacerated, his spleen was ruptured and had to be surgically removed. It was so badly damaged that it wasn't even in his body anymore. When they tried to save him, they had no choice but to take it out.

Charles was an organ donor. He had marked it on his driver's license, believing that if anything ever happened to him, his organs could help save someone else's life.

But that wasn't possible. Not a single organ could be harvested. The damage was too severe.

As I sat with that reality, I knew that no courtroom, no verdict, and no amount of justice could bring my son back.

CHOOSING FORGIVENESS– A DECISION, NOT A FEELING

I didn't wake up one morning and suddenly feel ready to forgive. It was a decision I had to make, over and over again. Some days, I felt strong in my choice. Other days, anger would creep back in, and I had to pray even harder. Forgiveness didn't mean forgetting. It didn't mean excusing. It didn't even mean that I would ever understand why this happened. It simply meant that I was trusting God to heal what I could not. I had to forgive, not because Garrett deserved it, but because my soul needed it.

MY MESSAGE TO ANYONE STRUGGLING TO FORGIVE

If you're reading this and struggling with forgiveness, I want you to know that I see you. I understand the pain of injustice. But I also want you to know that forgiveness is not about them—it's about you.

It's about releasing yourself from the burden of hate. It's about finding peace in God's hands.

As I have previously mentioned, I am not the same person I was before Charles was taken from me. The loss changed me forever. But in the process God showed me that even in my deepest sorrow, there is still redemption, still hope, still a future filled with grace. And for that I am undeniably grateful.

LETTING GO OF BITTERNESS

"Let all bitterness and wrath and anger and clamor and slander be put away from you, along with all malice. Be kind to one another, tenderhearted, forgiving one another, as God in Christ forgave you."

Ephesians 4:31-32

REFLECTION:

Bitterness may feel justified, but it only traps us in the past. True freedom comes when we release resentment and embrace the love and kindness of Christ. We forgive because we have been forgiven.

PRAYER:

"God, help me to let go of bitterness and replace it with Your peace. I want to be free from anger and resentment. Teach me to extend the same grace that You have shown me. Amen."

CHAPTER EIGHT

THE MOMENT OF EMBRACE

Forgiveness is an embrace. It's a wrapping of arms around another, pulling them close, and releasing the weight of pain and resentment.

I will never forget the day the trial ended, almost like it was yesterday. As we walked out of the Courtroom, we praised and gave glory to God for once again the victory that He had given us. Everyone was talking in the hallway; as we were talking to the DA and getting ready to leave, Garrett's family was standing around, and when I walked by, I looked at his mother; I knew she had lost Garrett's twin brother that year. I stopped and said to her, *"I am so sorry for your loss."*

Her reaction was immediate. She broke down in tears, sobbing in my arms for nearly fifteen minutes. Through her tears, she apologized, expressed her sorrow for what had happened, and talked about her son. She said, "During the first trial, I had lost my husband, and now seven years later, I have lost my son."

I embraced her with the love of God. I felt God's love in my heart for her. It was not a human reaction—it was God's grace and mercy working through me. I told her I would pray for her, that I forgave her, and that everything would be okay.

TRUE FORGIVENESS TRANSCENDS RACE

Imagine feeling empathy, compassion, and love at the same time. Amid my pain, I found empathy and compassion for her, even as I grappled with the racial tensions surrounding my son's murder. Empathy is the ability to understand and share another person's feelings. Compassion means "to suffer together."

Among emotion researchers, compassion is the feeling that arises when one is confronted with another's suffering and feels motivated to relieve that suffering.

God's love is often called Agape, a Greek word in the New Testament. Agape describes God's fatherly love for humanity and the reciprocal love humans express toward God. In Scripture, Agape love is portrayed as the highest and most selfless form of love, transcending all others.

With racism being such a critical issue in our world right now, you can imagine that out of all the years since my son was murdered, the racial aspect stood out more than anything else in my mind. The fact that my son was African American and her son was Caucasian became a significant point for our family, especially given the racial tensions that persist today and the fact that her son used the "N" word.

Oh, but the love of God, in the spirit of forgiveness and being able to let go and realize and know that God is bigger than anything that happens in our lives. When we're faced with trauma, it doesn't seem like He's bigger because the trauma is magnified more in our finite minds. We're human with our human thoughts.

But the one thing I realized through this whole situation was that God is bigger than what my family and I were going through. After Garrett asked for forgiveness during the trial, I searched the California State Prison's website, found his location, and sent him an encouragement card. Not long after that, Garrett sent me a letter thanking me for the card and asking for my forgiveness.

I shared Christ with Garrett; at some point, he accepted Christ as his Savior. It has always been about Christ and building a Kingdom legacy. Though I lost my son and will always carry the ache of his absence, I've come to understand that sharing Christ— even with the person who took his life—was part of something far greater than myself. It was a testament to God's grace and power working through me, and for that, I give Him all the glory.

Garrett started writing me letters, reading the Bible I sent him, sharing our story, and talking about forgiveness. Only God could do this.

September 18, 2022

"Dear Mrs. Briggs, I read 2 Corinthians 4:9, Micah 7:8, Isaiah 43:2 and that made me feel so much better about myself. When I killed Charles I tried to find out why I had so much hate and anger in my heart. I blamed your son for what I did and I was a coward!"

—Garrett

There were steps I had to take, and I could only take those steps through prayer, acknowledging God, and asking God to help me to press forward, move beyond race, and pass the fact that we had to go through another trial. Despite what was said and the negativity expressed, I still had to depend on God. I had to continue to believe in God and what He said He would do. Honestly, I look forward to hearing from Garrett. It's incredible to me that I feel the way I do.

God will blow your mind. Never in my finite mind could I be able to write the young man who murdered my son. Only God, who is infinite, could cause such a reaction.

"O the depth of the riches, both of the wisdom and knowledge of God! How unsearchable are his judgments and his ways

past finding out! For who hath known the mind of the Lord? or who hath been his counselor?"

Romans 11:33-34 (KJV)

November 25, 2022

"Mrs. Briggs, can I ask you a question? Does your family disagree with us writing and talking to each other? I was thinking about that when I was in the hospital. I mean I completely understand if they don't. What I did, how I thought and acted was evil and horrible. God saved me and gave me the courage to ask for your forgiveness, Please tell your family, I am so sorry, and I know the pain I caused. I hope I can get the chance to tell them myself and hear what they have to say to me—if that's what they would like to do."

Love, Garrett

It has been a journey to forgiveness because of the many things we have to press through. When we go on a journey, there are many obstacles we may face sometimes. Forgiveness is a choice; I choose to forgive because there is freedom that comes with forgiving. I realize when it came to forgiving Garret for murdering Charles, it was easy to do, but what about the small things that have been done to me as well. "It's the little foxes that spoil the vine," is a phrase from the Song of Solomon 2:15 (KJV), and it metaphorically means that seemingly insignificant problems or issues, like "little foxes," can cause major damage if not addressed.

LOVE YOUR ENEMIES

"But I say to you who hear, Love your enemies, do good to those who hate you."

Luke 6:27

REFLECTION:

Loving those who have wronged us is one of the hardest commands Jesus gave, yet it is what sets us apart as His followers. When we extend love where hate once lived, we reflect the heart of Christ. Forgiveness is an act of love—not just for others, but for ourselves.

PRAYER:

"Father, this is hard. Loving those who have hurt me feels impossible, but I know You call me to a higher standard. Change my heart, Lord. Help me to love as You love. Amen."

CHAPTER NINE

A LESSON IN FORGIVENESS: WHAT THE BRIGGS FAMILY TAUGHT ME

A PERSONAL NOTE

What Garrett Adams did was, in my mind, unforgivable. I never got to meet Charles, of course. But like the victims in all my cases, I got a sense of who he was by talking to the people who loved him. And I could tell Charles was an amazing person. You could tell from the love of his family, his friends, and everyone who knew him. You could tell from their fierce dedication to his case. Most of all, you could tell by the way he died: helping a complete stranger because he knew she was in distress and possibly in danger.

I had no sympathy for Garrett Adams. He was a bully. He beat up his girlfriend, Bernadette. When Charles stood up for her, Garrett tried to be the "alpha male" by fighting Charles. When Garrett couldn't beat Charles in a fair fight, he ran off to get a weapon so he could beat Charles in an unfair fight. And even though Charles was de-escalating and walking away, Garrett shot him. For the absolute worst of reasons: because he felt small compared to who Charles was.

And probably (maybe only subconsciously) because Charles was Black. I was glad when the jury convicted Garrett of murder. Sentencing hearings are always rough. It's hard to listen to any family talk about the unthinkable pain that a murderer causes. It's especially hard with a family like the Briggs family, who I had grown to know and appreciate their love for Charles. After they were done speaking, I think everyone in the room was emotionally raw. I know I was.

When Garrett's lawyer said that Garrett wanted to say something, I braced myself. I was afraid he was going to offer some justification for what he did or try to avoid responsibility, or something like that. Instead, there was almost a small miracle: Garrett apologized, saying he thought about what he did every day and that he would do anything to take it back. I was really surprised. This was someone that I would have bet a lot of money was self-centered and had no real insight into what he had done.

It was a lesson to me that I still try and remember. But that wasn't the biggest lesson I learned that day - because as Garrett finished apologizing, I heard the Briggs family saying to him, "I forgive you." I was floored by that. I didn't have it in my heart to forgive him. I walked over to Garrett and told him what the family had said in case he couldn't hear it from where he was. I didn't have that amount of grace in my heart, but they did, and I hoped it would do some good.

I still can't forgive him. But I'm trying to learn the lesson the Briggs family put out there for all of us that day."

—Ryan Williams
(Writing in my personal capacity, not on behalf of the District Attorney's Office)–Ryan Williams

TRUSTING GOD'S JUSTICE

"Beloved, never avenge yourselves, but leave it to the wrath of God, for it is written, 'Vengeance is mine, I will repay, says the Lord.'"

Romans 12:19

REFLECTION:

Forgiving does not mean ignoring justice. It means trusting God to handle what we cannot. He sees every wrong and will bring justice in His time. Letting go of the need for revenge allows us to walk in peace, knowing that God is in control.

PRAYER:

"Lord, I release my desire for vengeance. I trust You to bring justice in Your way and in Your time. Help me to rest in Your promises. Amen."

CHAPTER TEN

GRACE BEHIND BARS: A MOTHER'S DAY OF RECKONING

March 6, 2023

"Dear Mrs. Briggs, Thank you. You really helped me get back up and not quit on myself.

Love, Garrett

I look forward to receiving Garrett's letters after receiving notice they're coming in the mail. I get them from the mailbox, retreat to the room, and read. It's just amazing what God can do.

One thing I had to do was to continue to pray that God would not let my heart be filled with hatred, and I'm not going to say that there weren't times when I felt a certain way because it was the truth. Still, I had to do what I said earlier constantly. I had to be very intentional about my prayers and not wanting vengeance. God says in His Word that vengeance belongs to Him. Initially, I realized that losing Charles, as tragic as it was and that it was so much bigger than me. It's about sharing Christ. So, I pray for Garrett and his family and continue to do so.

After a year of corresponding with Garrett, I decided to apply to the California Prison System to visit him. In July 2023, they approved my application. We planned to meet face-to-face on August 18, 2023. However, I soon learned there was a different process for visiting because I was a victim or part of a victim's family. That's when I discovered there was a vetting process, and Garrett and I had to go through an alternative procedure. I received a call from Sacramento and was introduced to the Mend Collaborative.

After contacting the Mend Collaborative, we began meeting in the Lancaster-Palmdale area in October 2023. From that point until June or July 2024, I participated in meetings with the Collaborative while they also met with Garrett separately. It wasn't until July 18, 2024 that Garrett and I could finally meet face-to-face.

The Victim Offender Dialogue (VOD) program, offered by the California Department of Corrections and Rehabilitation (CDCR), opens for healing and accountability. This restorative justice initiative brings victims and offenders together, creating a space where closure and accountability intertwined. After a thorough vetting process with the Mend Collaborative, a Los Angeles-based nonprofit dedicated to fostering healing and transformation, I was approved for the meeting. Mend Collaborative aims to bridge survivors and those responsible for harm through high-quality restorative justice practices. They assured me that this process would prepare both Garrett and me for what was to come.

Garrett Adams and Charlotte Perry-Briggs

THE DAY OF THE MEETING

On July 18, 2024, Rebecca Weiler, Mend Collaborative's director, picked me up at 7 a.m. for the 130-mile drive to the California Correctional Institute in Tehachapi. Sleep had eluded me the night before, and my heart was heavy with uncertainty about what lay ahead. Yet, I was carried by the prayers of my pastors, Apostle Fred and Pastor Linda Hodge, my Living Praise Church family, and other prayer warriors. I prayed for God's presence, asking Him to guide the meeting and bring Him glory.

After passing rigorous security checks, we walked through several buildings before arriving at a small, unassuming room. A table sat in the back, where Garrett and his support person were waiting alongside a Mend Collaborative restorative justice practitioner. A correctional officer sat silently by the door. Rebecca and I entered the room with my support person. There were six of us, and the atmosphere was thick with emotion.

Garrett rose to greet me, extending a tentative handshake. Meeting his gaze, I told him, "You look well." I could see the nervousness in his eyes, a reflection of the storm within us both. Then, unexpectedly, he handed me a handcrafted long-stem paper rose in my favorite color, pink. Although we had had several phone conversations and corresponding letters, I don't recall ever sharing that detail with him. The gesture overwhelmed me, and tears flowed from my eyes. The room grew quiet as we wept together, joined by the tears of those supporting us.

That simple gift—a fragile rose—touched a deep place in my heart. It reminded me of my late pastor's words: "What comes from the heart reaches the heart, and what comes from the Spirit reaches the Spirit." At that moment, I felt Garrett's remorse. The rose reminded me of Charles, who often surprised me with flowers, his love etched in every petal.

Garrett had shared his journey with the Pawsitive Change Program with me, where incarcerated individuals train rescue dogs. Through this initiative, he learned responsibility, patience, and empathy—qualities he admitted he had lacked for much of his life. The program rehabilitates the dogs and fosters emotional growth and a sense of purpose in the inmates. At one point, I suggested Garrett bring Lucky, the dog he was training, into the room. The emotions in that space were overwhelming, and Lucky's presence provided a calming balm.

Our meeting lasted five hours, from 9:00 a.m. to 2:00 p.m., and the time felt endless and fleeting. We talked about Charles—his life, character, and the void his death left in our family. Garrett, in his trembling voice, admitted, *"Charles didn't deserve to die like that. He was protecting someone he didn't even know."* He told me he had asked others about Charles to understand the man he had wronged.

When I asked Garrett the question that had burned in my heart for years—why he referred to my son with the racial slur, the "N" word, after killing him—his tears returned. *"Mrs. Briggs,"* he began, his voice breaking, *"I was taught to hate Black people. That's all I know. My brother and I fought with Black kids all the time after we moved to Lancaster. I was drunk that night, and when I drank, my anger spiraled out of control. Sorry, it isn't enough, but I think about Charles daily. I wish I could take it all back."*

His honesty was piercing. Garrett spoke of a childhood marred by dysfunction—a father consumed by alcoholism, a home lost to financial ruin, and a descent into substance abuse. Though he had been sober for months, the weight of his past was evident. My support person and I initially wondered if his remorse was genuine or a calculated attempt to display good behavior. But as the day unfolded, his raw vulnerability dissolved our doubts.

We shared a meal, took photos, and continued to speak from the heart. By the time we left, I felt a profound sense of closure. Garrett's words and actions confirmed what we had long believed: Charles died protecting others, embodying the selflessness that defined him.

A TURNING POINT

Meeting Garrett was a turning point. It confirmed my family's grief and affirmed our memories of who Charles was. While every victim's journey differs, this experience was a positive step in my healing. I encourage anyone considering such a dialogue to pursue it through an organization like Mend Collaborative. Their meticulous preparation ensured the meeting's success, providing both parties with the tools and support needed.

Through programs like the Pawsitive Change Program, which pairs incarcerated individuals with rescue dogs, Garrett had learned empathy, patience, and responsibility. His growth was evident, and it gave me hope that redemption was possible.

By the end of the meeting, I felt a profound sense of peace. Forgiveness had set both of us free.

WALKING IN FREEDOM

"So if the Son sets you free, you will be free indeed."

John 8:36

REFLECTION:

Forgiveness isn't just about the other person—it's about your freedom. When we forgive, we release ourselves from the chains of anger, pain, and resentment. Jesus came so that we could walk in complete freedom. Today, choose to step into that freedom.

PRAYER:

"Jesus, I want to walk in the freedom that forgiveness brings. Thank You for setting me free. Help me to live each day with a heart open to grace, love, and healing. Amen."

CONCLUSION

Forgiveness is not a destination; it is a journey I continue to walk every day. Through God's grace, I have found healing and purpose in the face of loss.

My prayer is that this story inspires others to seek healing, to embrace forgiveness, and to trust in God's plan, even in the midst of indescribable pain.

Charles' legacy lives on in every act of love, every story shared, and every life touched by his memory. Though his life was tragically cut short, his story is one of faith, resilience, and the transformative power of grace.

January 24, 2025

Good morning. I'm sorry my response was late; I got sidetracked yesterday. But I think doing a book club would be great. I asked a few facilitators here on my tier and they're both going to help me get something going. I want to also thank you for being so considerate and careful about putting things in your book that might cause me harm or issues in the future. We both need to understand that this is going to be hard for some people to deal with our story, and the feelings they're going to have. It will open a lot of stuff that some people don't know how to cope with, and putting a picture of us and showing everyone our relationship is created through our love for Christ and understanding of what happened was horrible, but learning and showing how to heal on both sides will help whoever reads this book. I give u my word. I will help you with whatever you and your team need. I truly care about u and want nothing but the best for you and your family, and I will always be there for you guys. No matter what. I will not let evil thoughts or feelings from other people interfere with our mission. Have a great day, Mrs. Briggs!!

Garrett

The power of grace—grace that mends, grace that transforms, and grace that allows us to see beyond the pain to the possibility of redemption

—Anonymous

Charles Emmanuel Briggs-Age 23

ACKNOWLEDGMENTS

To my family: Thank you for your unwavering love and support—they have been my anchor throughout this.

To my spiritual leaders, Apostle and Pastor Linda Hodge: Your guidance and covering have been a constant source of strength and encouragement.

To our extended family, united through the life and legacy of Charles: Your love and connection mean more than words can express.

To Garrett Adams: Thank you for encouraging me to share this story—it's a testament to the power of redemption and grace.

ABOUT THE AUTHOR

Charlotte Perry-Briggs is a compassionate and inspirational woman and a first-time author whose life is a testament to resilience, faith, and the power of forgiveness. Her journey is deeply rooted in her unwavering commitment to her faith, family, and community.

Charlotte accepted Jesus Christ as her Lord and Savior as a teenager, a decision that would become the cornerstone of her life. Her faith has guided her through life's greatest challenges, shaping her deep passion for helping others. Whether through acts of kindness or advocacy, Charlotte has dedicated her life to making a meaningful impact on those around her.

In 2014, Charlotte's life changed forever when her beloved son, Charles, was tragically murdered. This inconceivable loss became a defining moment in her life. Instead of succumbing to despair, Charlotte found strength in her faith and transformed her grief into a powerful force for good. She became a Domestic Violence Advocate, using her voice and experience to bring hope and healing to others impacted by violence.

Charlotte's advocacy extends beyond words. She has supported countless individuals and families in need by providing meal cards, clothing, and Christmas gifts, ensuring they feel seen and cared for even in their darkest moments.

Recognizing the need for systemic change, Charlotte has partnered with two transformative organizations to share her story and inspire others:

- The Mend Collaborative: This nonprofit organization focuses on restorative justice and healing for individuals and communities affected by violence. Through her partnership, Charlotte addresses the needs of victims, survivors, and offenders, fostering understanding, accountability, and healing in profound and life-changing ways.

- The GRIP Training Institute (Guiding Rage Into Power): This nonprofit is dedicated to transforming violence and suffering into opportunities for learning and healing. Through GRIP, Charlotte shares her journey of forgiveness and reconciliation, offering hope to those seeking redemption and renewal.

Charlotte's life is a beacon of hope, showing that faith and love can prevail even in the face of devastating loss. Her powerful message of forgiveness and healing inspires others to overcome adversity and find peace. Through her advocacy, she is honoring the memory of her son, Charles, and creating a legacy that brings light to those in need.

Charlotte is an active member of Living Praise Christian Church, with campuses in Palmdale and North Hollywood, California. Her church family has been a source of encouragement and spiritual strength, empowering her to live out her purpose.

Her story is one of enduring love and faith. She and her husband, Charlie Briggs, Jr., have been married for over 40 years. Together, they have raised three daughters and one son, who transitioned to be with the Lord. They have built a life centered on their shared faith and commitment to serving others. Charlotte and her husband reside in Southern California, where Charlotte continues her work as an advocate and mentor.

RESOURCE & SUPPORT SECTION

Finding Strength, Support, and Healing Through Faith

1. **Books on Forgiveness, Healing, and Faith**

Below are a few books to continue your journey with books from trusted Christian authors. Here are some recommendations:

- *Forgive: Why Should I and How Can I?* — Timothy Keller
- *Total Forgiveness* — R.T. Kendall
- *The Bait of Satan: Living Free from the Deadly Trap of Offense* — John Bevere
- *Choosing Forgiveness: Your Journey to Freedom* — Nancy Leigh DeMoss
- *Healing Is a Choice* — Stephen Arterburn

2. **Bible Verses on Forgiveness & Healing**

These scriptures can serve as a foundation for readers who want to study forgiveness further.

- **Forgiveness:**
    - Matthew 6:14-15 — *"For if you forgive others their trespasses, your heavenly Father will also forgive you."*
    - Colossians 3:13 — *"Bear with each other and forgive one another if any of you has a grievance against someone. Forgive as the Lord forgave you."*
    - Luke 23:34 — *"Father, forgive them, for they know not what they do."*

- **Healing & Comfort:**
    - Psalm 34:18 — *"The Lord is close to the brokenhearted and saves those who are crushed in spirit."*
    - Isaiah 41:10 — *"Fear not, for I am with you; be not dismayed, for I am your God. I will strengthen you, I will help you, I will uphold you with my righteous right hand."*

3. **Counseling and Faith-Based Support Groups**

For readers seeking personal support, consider adding Christian counseling and faith-based organizations:

- **Grief and Trauma Support:**
    - *GriefShare* — www.griefshare.org (Christian-based grief support groups)

- *Focus on the Family* — www.focusonthefamily.com (Christian counseling & family support)
- *Stephen Ministries* — www.stephenministries.org (Church-based caregiving and support)

- **Forgiveness & Reconciliation Resources:**
  - *The Forgiveness Project* — www.theforgivenessproject.com
  - *Peacemaker Ministries* — www.peacemakerministries.org (Biblical conflict resolution)

4. **Christian Counseling & Mental Health Resources**

For those struggling with grief, trauma, or emotional pain, professional help is available:

- **American Association of Christian Counselors (AACC)** — www.aacc.net

- **Christian Counseling & Educational Foundation (CCEF)** — www.ccef.org

- **National Christian Counselors Association** — www.ncca.org

5. **ReEvolution www.reevolutiongroup.org Rafael Cuevas— Cuevas@reevp;itopmgrpi[/cp**

An organization dedicated to creating restorative community through advocacy, in-prison programs, and reentry initiatives.

www.ingramcontent.com/pod-product-compliance
Lightning Source LLC
Chambersburg PA
CBHW071527120626
46550CB00006B/2383